William Wallace Tooker

John Eliot's First Indian Teacher and Interpreter

William Wallace Tooker

John Eliot's First Indian Teacher and Interpreter

ISBN/EAN: 9783744712781

Printed in Europe, USA, Canada, Australia, Japan

Cover: Foto ©Thomas Meinert / pixelio.de

More available books at **www.hansebooks.com**

JOHN ELIOT'S

FIRST INDIAN TEACHER AND
INTERPRETER

COCKENOE-DE-LONG ISLAND

AND

The Story of His Career from the Early Records

BY

WILLIAM WALLACE TOOKER

*Member of the Long Island Historical Society, Anthropological
Society of Washington, etc., etc.*

✠

" He was the first that I made use of to teach me words
and to be my interpreter."—*Eliot's Letter*, 2, 12, 1648.

✠

LONDON:
HENRY STEVENS' SON AND STILES.
1896

JOHN ELIOT'S

FIRST INDIAN TEACHER AND
INTERPRETER

COCKENOE-DE-LONG ISLAND

AND

The Story of His Career from the Early Records

BY

WILLIAM WALLACE TOOKER

*Member of the Long Island Historical Society, Anthropological
Society of Washington, etc., etc.*

✣

" He was the first that I made use of to teach me words
and to be my interpreter."—*Eliot's Letter*, 2, 12, 1648.

✣

LONDON:

HENRY STEVENS' SON AND STILES.

1896

INTRODUCTION.

This little work is a brief résumé of the career of an Indian of Long Island, who, from his exceptional knowledge of the English language, his traits of character, and strong personality, was recognized as a valuable coadjutor and interpreter by many of our first English settlers. These personal attributes were also known and appreciated by the inhabitants of some parts of Connecticut and Massachusetts, by the Commissioners of the United Colonies of New England, and by the Governor of the Colony of New York, all of whom found occasion for his services in their transactions with the Indians. The facts which I shall present in their chronological order, and the strong circumstantial evidence adduced therefrom, will indicate the reasons why I have unraveled the

viii   *Introduction.*

threads of this Indian's life from the weft of the past, and why the recital of his career should be the theme of a special essay, and worthy of a distinctive chapter in the aboriginal, as well as in the Colonial, history of Long Island.

WILLIAM WALLACE TOOKER.

SAG HARBOR, L. I., *March*, 1896.

C.A.Harper

COCKENOE-DE-LONG ISLAND.

THE victory of Captain John Mason and Captain John Underhill over the Pequots on the hills of Mystic, in 1637, in its results was far greater than that of Wellington on the field of Waterloo. This fact will impress itself in indelible characters on the minds of those who delve into the historical truths connected with the genesis of our settlements, so wide spreading were the fruits of this victory. As the native inhabitants of the eastern part of Long Island and the adjacent islands were subjects of, and under tribute to, these dreaded Pequots,[1] they were more or less disturbed by the issues of the after conflicts which ensued in hunting out the fleeing survivors. But as two of the Long Island Sachems, Yoco, the Sachem of Shelter Island, and Wyandanch, the Sachem of Montauk, through the mediation of their friend Lion Gardiner came three days after the fight, and placed themselves under the protection of the victors,[2] and, as the latter with his men assisted Captain Stoughton during the finale at the "Great Swamp,"[3] beyond New Haven, they did not feel the effects so severely as did the immediate allies of the Pequots.

[1] "The Pequots were a very warlike and potent people about forty years since, (1624) at which time they were in their meridian. Their chief Sachem held dominion over divers petty Sagamores, as over part of Long Island, over the Mohegans, and over the Sagamores of Quinapak, yea, over all the people that dwelt on Connecticut river, and over some of the most southerly inhabitants of the Nipmuk country about Quinabang."—Gookin's History.

Gardiner's Relation of the Pequot Wars (Lion Gardiner and his Descendants, by C. C. Gardiner, 1890) : " Then said he, (Waiandance) I will go to my brother, for he is the great Sachem of Long Island, and if we may have peace and trade with you, we will give you tribute as we did the Pequits."

[2] Relation of the Pequot Wars (Lion Gardiner and his Descendants, by C. C. Gardiner, 1890), p. 17.

[3] *Ibid.*, pp. 17, 18.

Many of the younger Indians captured in this
war, especially those taken in Connecticut, were
carried to Boston, and there sold into slavery,
or distributed around the country into a limited
period of servitude [4]—a period generally termi-
nating when the individual so bound had
arrived at the age of twenty-five.

Among those so captured and allotted was a
young Indian of Long Island, who became a
servant in the family of a prominent citizen of
Dorchester, Mass.,[5] a sergeant in the same war,
and therefore possibly his captor. This young
Indian having been a native of Long Island,
and on a visit, was perhaps a reason why he was
detained in the colony, for the young male
Pequots, we are told, were all expatriated.[6]

[4] Morton's New England's Memorial, 1669, Reprint 1855, p. 131 :
" We send the male children to Bermuda by Mr. William Pierce, and
the women and maid children are disposed about in the towns."

[5] " Richard Collacot was a prominent man in Dorchester. He had been
a sergeant in the Pequot War, and held also at various times the offices
of Selectman and of Representative." In 1641, with two associates, he
was licensed by the Governor of Massachusetts, to trade with the Indians,
also to receive all wampum due for any tribute from Block Island, Long
Island Pequots or any other Indians.—Archæologia Americana, vol. vii.
pp. 67, 434.

[6] New England's Memorial, 1669. Reprint 1855, p. 131.

In proof of these findings of fact we have the testimony of the Rev. John Eliot, than whom no one is better known for his labors in behalf of the spiritual welfare of the Indians of eastern Massachusetts, and for his works in their language, including that monumental work which went through two editions, Eliot's Indian Bible. It is thought that Eliot began his study of the Indian language about 1643, but it is possible that he began much earlier. In a letter dated February 12, 1649 (2–12–'48), he wrote:

"There is an Indian living with Mr. Richard Calicott of Dorchester, who was taken in the Pequott warres, though belonging to Long Island. This Indian is ingenious, can read, and I taught him to write, which he quickly learnt, though I know not what use he now maketh of it. He was the first that I made use of to teach me words, and to be my interpreter."

At the end of his Indian grammar (printed at Cambridge in 1666) Mr. Eliot gives us an account of his method of learning the language and some more information in regard to this young Long Island Indian. He writes: "I

THE

Indian Primer;

OR,

The way of training up of our
Indian Youth in the good
knowledge of God, in the
knowledge of the Scriptures
and in an ability to Reade.

Composed by J. E.

2 Tim. 3 14, 15. Qut ken nag-
wuttcanſh niſh nahtuntnaaziſh
k. h poſkontnnaaiſh, wab: adt
noh ſabtuhtanonadt
15, Kah wutch hunmukki ſuin-
neat kowabteo wutneetupaca-
tammé waſſ ykwhongiſh, &c.

Cambridge, Printed 1669.

FAC-SIMILE OF THE TITLE-PAGE OF THE PRIMER OF 1669.

have now finished what I shall do at present;
and in a word or two to satisfie the prudent En-
quirer how I found out these new ways of grammar, which no other Learned Language (so
farre as I know) useth ; I thus inform him : God
first put into my heart a compassion over their
poor souls, and a desire to teach them to know
Christ, and to bring them into his kingdome.
Then presently I found out, (by Gods wise
providence) a pregnant witted young man, who
had been a servant in an English house, who
pretty well understood our Language, better
than he could speak it, and well understood his
own Language, and hath a clear pronuncia-
tion ; Him I made my Interpreter. By his help
I translated the Commandments, the Lords
Prayer, and many Texts of Scripture : also I
compiled both exhortations and prayers by his
help, I diligently marked the difference of their
grammar from ours ; when I found the way of
them, I would pursue a Word, a Noun, a Verb,
through all the variations I could think of.
We must sit still and look for Miracles ; up, and
be doing, and the Lord will be with thee.

Prayer and pains through Faith in Christ Jesus, will do anything."

In 1646 Mr. Eliot began to preach to the Indians in their own tongue. About the middle of September he addressed a company of the natives in the wigwam of Cutshamoquin, the Sachem of Neponset, within the limits of Dorchester. His next attempt was made among the Indians of another place, "those of Dorchester mill not regarding any such thing." On the 28th of October he delivered a sermon before a large number assembled in the principal wigwam of a chief named Waban, situated four or five miles from Roxbury, on the south side of the Charles river, near Watertown mill, now in the township of Newton. The services were commenced with prayer, which, as Mr. Shepard relates, " now was in English, being not so farre acquainted with the Indian language as to expresse our hearts herein before God or them." After Mr. Eliot had finished his discourse, which was in the Indian language, he "asked them if they understood all that which was already spoken, and whether all of them in the wigwam did understand, or onely some few? and they answered to this question with multitude of voyces, that they all of them did understand all that which was then spoken to them." He then replied to a number of questions which they propounded to him, "*borrowing now and then some small helpe from the Interpreter whom wee brought with us, and who could oftentimes expresse our minds more distinctly than any of us could.*" Three more meetings were held at this place in November and December of the same year, accounts of which are given by the Rev. Thomas Shepard in the tract, entitled, *The Day-Breaking, if not the Sun-Rising of the Gospell with the Indians in New England,* London, 1647. I have quoted these letters and remarks from the interesting notes on John Eliot's life, contributed to Pilling's Algonquian Bibliography,[7] by Mr. Wilberforce Eames of the Lenox Library, New York.

As Mr. Eliot in the foregoing letters has testified to what extent he was indebted to this young Indian, there can arise no question whatever as to the great influence which the

[7] Pp. 176, 117.

instruction and information thus obtained must
have had on his subsequent knowledge of the
Indian language. It also indicates how close
an affinity and how little dialectical difference
existed between the language spoken by the
eastern Long Island Indians and that of the
Natick or Massachusetts Indians to which his
works are credited. In fact, the identity
between these two dialects is closer than exists
between either of them and the Narragansett
of Roger Williams, as can be easily proven
by comparison. Again, Eliot, in his grammar
twenty years afterward, as I have before quoted,
by so confessing his obligation to his young
teacher to the total exclusion of Job Nesutan,
who took his place,[8] shows how he appreciated
the instruction first imparted. Eliot having
written, in the winter of 1648–49, that he taught

[8] Eliot wrote October 21, 1650 : "I have one already who can write,
so that I can read his writing well, and he (with some paines and teaching)
can read mine." The native here referred to was, without doubt, Job
Nesutan, who had taken the place of the Long Island Indian, Eliot's
first instructor in the language. He is mentioned by Gookin in the
History of the Christian Indians as follows : "In this expedition
[July, 1675] one of our principal soldiers of the praying Indians was
slain, a valiant and stout man named Job Nesutan ; he was a very good

this Indian how to read and to write, which he
quickly learned, though he knew not what use
he then made of the knowledge, it becomes
apparent to all that he had then departed, to
Eliot's great regret, from the scene of Eliot's
labors in Massachusetts; and, as seems to have
been the case, had returned to the home of his
ancestors on Long Island sometime between
the fall of 1646, when he was with Eliot in
Waban's wigwam, and the winter of 1649, when
Eliot wrote.[9] Whether his time as a servant
had expired, or whether he longed for the
country of his youth and childhood, we perhaps
shall never learn.

At this point the interesting question arises,
Can we identify any one of the Long Island
Indians of this period with the " interpreter" or
" pregnant witted young man " of John Eliot?

linguist in the English tongue, and was Mr. Eliot's assistant and interpreter in his translations of the Bible, and other books of the Indian
language."—Bibliography of the Alqonquian Language ; Pilling (Eames's
Notes, p. 127).

[9] In the summer of 1647 Eliot visited some more remote Indians about
Cape Cod and toward the Merrimack river, where he improved the
opportunity by preaching to them.   It is probable that about this time
his interpreter left Dorchester.

Here it must be conceded that the evidence is entirely circumstantial and not direct; but withal so strong and so convincing as to make me a firm believer in its truth, as I shall set it forth before you.

I shall begin my exposition with the Indian deed of the East Hampton township, dated April 29, 1648,[10] where we find, by the power acquired by the grantees from the Farrett mortgage of 1641,[11] that Thomas Stanton made a purchase from the Indians for Theophilus Eaton, Esq., Governor of the Colony of New Haven, and Edward Hopkins, Esq., Governor of the Colony of Connecticut, and their associates "for all that tract of land lyinge from the bounds of the Inhabitants of Southampton, unto the East side of *Napeak*, next unto *Meuntacut* high land, with the whole breadth from

[10] East Hampton Records, vol. i. pp. 3, 45 ; Chronicles of East Hampton ; p. 113.

[11] Thompson's History of Long Island, vol. ii. p. 311, 312, 313. The rights acquired by this mortgage are very explicit, and began as soon the same was sealed and delivered. Its bearing on the purchases from the Indians by the Colonies of Connecticut seems to have been overlooked by all our historians.

sea to sea, etc.," this conveyance is signed by the four Sachems of Eastern Long Island—to wit: *Poggatacut,*[12] the Sachem of *Munhansett;* *Wyandanch,*[13] the Sachem of *Meuntacut;* *Momoweta,*[14] the Sachem of *Corchake;* *Nowedonah,*[15] the Sachem of *Shinecok,* and their marks are witnessed by *Cheekanoo,* who is thereon stated to have been "*their Interpreter.*"[16]

[12] This is the only instance in the early records of Long Island where we find the old Sachem of Shelter Island called *Poggatacut.* I believe it to have been rather the name of a place where he lived, either at Cockles Harbor, or on Menantic Creek, Shelter Island. *Poggat-ac-ut* = *Pohqutack-ut,* "at the divided or double place." Cockles Harbor is protected on the north by two Islands, which during low tides are one Island. It was probably the sheltered condition of this harbor which gave the island its Indian name as well as its English. It was at this locality that Govert Loockmans purchased two geese from the chief Rochbou [Yoco] in 1647. —Colonial History of New York, vol. xiv. p. 94.

[13] *Wyandanch* = *Wayan-taunche,* " the wise speaker or talker."

[14] *Momoweta* = *Mohmô-wetuô,* " he gathereth or brings together in his house."

[15] *Nowedonah* = *N'owi-dônoh,* "I seek him," or " I go to seek him." This Sachem was formerly called *Witaneymen* or *Weenagamin,* and he probably changed his name when he went to spy out the enemies of the Dutch in 1645 (Colonial History of New York, vol. xiv. p. 60), see also Thompson's Long Island, vol. i. p. 365, Plymouth Colonial Records, vol. ix. p. 18, where he is called *Weenakamin, i. e.,* " bitter berry."

[16] The original of this deed has been stolen from the Town Clerk's office at East Hampton ; consequently, I am unable to verify the spelling of these names. On some copies of this deed this name is printed

Here we find confronting us, not only a remarkable, but a very unusual circumstance, in
the fact that an Indian of Long Island, who is
called "*Cheekanoo*," is acting as an interpreter
for these four Sachems, together with Thomas
Stanton,[17] another well-known interpreter of the
Colonies, as an intermediary in making the purchase. It is very clear to me, and I think it
will be to all, that if this Indian was sufficiently
learned to speak English, and so intelligent as
to act as an interpreter, with all such a qualification would indicate, in 1648, the year before
Eliot commended his ingenious teacher, and
within the time he seems to have returned to
Long Island, he must have acquired his knowledge from someone who had taken great pains
in bestowing it, and that one must have been
John Eliot. We have found that Eliot does
not mention him by name in existing letters;
but, as before quoted, simply calls him his " In-

Cheetanoo; an evident error, for in no other instance do I find the *k* in
his name replaced by a *t*.

[17] See Pilling's Algonquian Bibliography (pp. 396, 397), for a brief
sketch of Thos. Stanton's career as an Interpreter to the Commissioners
of the United Colonies of New England.

terpreter "; therefore, let us learn how a translation of his Long Island appellation will bear on
this question.

This name, *Cheekanoo, Cockenoe, Chickino,
Chekkonnow,* or *Cockoo,*—no matter how varied
in the records of Long Island and elsewhere,
for every Town Clerk or Recorder, with but a
limited or no knowledge of the Indian tongue
and its true sounds, wrote down the name as it
suited him, and seldom twice alike even on the
same page,—finds its parallel sounds in the Massachusetts of both Eliot and Cotton, in the verb
kuhkinneau, or *kehkinnoo,* " he marks, observes,
takes knowledge, instructs, or imitates " ; [18]
hence, " he interprets," and therefore indicating
by a free translation "an interpreter or teacher";
this word in its primitive form occurs in all dialects of the same linguistic family—that is, the
Algonquian—in an infinite number of com-

[18] The root *kuhkoo* or *kehkoo,* has simply the idea of " mark " or a
"sign," which in Algonquian polysynthesis is modified according to its
grammatical affixes, and the sense of the passage used, when translated
into an alien tongue. But it must be remembered, however, that its
primary meaning was never lost to an Indian—a fact well known to all
students of Indian linguistics.

pounds, denoting "a scholar; teacher; a thing
signified; I say what he says, *i. e.*, repeat after
him," etc.[19]

These I may call inferential marks by the
wayside, and with what is to follow are surely
corroborative evidence strong enough to enable
me to assume that I am on the right trail, and
that "*Cheekanoo*" and John Eliot's young man
were one and the same individual. In its acceptance it becomes obvious that he must have
been so termed before the date of the East
Hampton conveyance, while still with Eliot in
Massachusetts. Indian personal names were
employed to denote some remarkable event in
their lives, and having been a teacher and an
interpreter of Eliot's, and continuing in the
same line afterward, which gave him greater
celebrity, it was natural that he should retain
the name throughout his life.

A little over two weeks after the East Hampton transaction, by a deed dated May 16, 1648[20]

[19] Compare the various derivates from the Nipissing (Cuoq) *kikina* and
kikino ; Otchipwe (Baraga) *kikino ;* Cree (Lacomb) *okiskino ;* Delaware
(Zeisberger) *kikino*, etc.

[20] Book of Deeds, vol. ii. p. 210, office of the Secretary of State, Albany,

(O. S.), *Mammawetough*, the Sachem of *Corchauge*, with the possible assistance of our interpreter, who, it seems to me, could not have been dispensed with on such an occasion, conveys *Hashamomuck* neck—which included all the land to the eastward of Pipe's Neck creek, in Southold town, on which the villages of Greenport, East Marion, and Orient are located, together with Plum Island—to Theophilus Eaton, Stephen Goodyeare, and Captain Malbow of New Haven. This is known as the Indian deed for the "Oyster Ponds," and while *Cheekanoo's* name does not appear on this copy of a copy, for the original has long been lost, it is possible that it may be disguised in the name of one of the witnesses, *Pitchamock*.

While we may infer from the foregoing documents that his services must have been necessarily in constant demand by the colonists in their interviews with the natives, during the four years following the making of these deeds,

N. Y. A copy of this deed, from a contemporary copy made by Richard Terry, then on sale at Dodd & Mead's, New York, was contributed to the Greenport Watchman by Wm. S. Pelletreau, June 6, 1891.

we do not find him again on record until February 25, 1652[21] (O. S., February 15, 1651), when he is identically employed as at East Hampton, by the proprietors of Norwalk, Conn., probably on the recommendation of the authorities at New Haven; and his name appears among the grantors, in two places on the Indian deed for the Norwalk plantation as "*Cockenoe-de-Long Island.*" But, as he did not sign the conveyance, it shows that he had no vested rights therein, but simply acted for the whites and Indians as their interpreter. From the possible fact that he perhaps erected his wigwam there during this winter and spring of 1651–52, thus giving it a distinctive appellation, an island in the Long Island sound off Westport, Conn., near the mouth of the Saugatuck river, bears his name in the possessive as "*Cockenoe's* Island" to this day, as will be noted by consulting a Coast Survey chart. That the name was bestowed in his time is proven by the record "that it was agreed (in 1672) that the said Island called Cockenoe is to

[21] Hall's Norwalk, p. 35.

lie common for the use of the town as all the other Islands are."[22] This island is one of the largest and most easterly of the group known as the " Norwalk Islands," or as they were designated by the early Dutch navigators, the Archipelago.[23] The fact that his name is displayed on this deed for Norwalk, and as the name for this island, has been a puzzle to many historians ; but that it does so appear is easily accounted for, when we know what his abilities were, and why he was there.

On September 2, 1652,[24] the fall of the year that he was at Norwalk, he appeared before the Commissioners of the United Colonies of New England, then assembled at Hartford, as their records bear witness in the following language : " Whereas we were informed by *Checkanoe* an Indian of *Menhansick* Island, on behalf of the

[22] Hall's Norwalk, p. 62.

[23] Another island of this group bears the personal name of an Indian who was called *Mamachimin* (Hall's Norwalk, pp. 30, 93, 97. He joined in the Indian deed to Roger Ludlow of Norwalk, February 26, 1640, corresponding to March 8, 1641). The name still survives, abbreviated to " *Chimons* Island."

[24] Colonial Records of Connecticut, vol. iv. p. 476.

Indian inhabitants of said island, that they are
disturbed in their possession by Captain Middleton and his agents, upon pretense of a purchase from Mr. Goodyeare of New Haven, who
bought the same of one Mr. Forrett, a scotch-
man, and by vertue thereof the said Indians
are threatened to be forced off the said island
and to seek an habitation where they can get
it ; the said Indians deny that they sold the
said island to the said Forrett; and that the
said Forrett was a poor man, not able to purchase it, but the said Indians gave to the said
Forrett some part of the said Island and marked
it out by some trees ; yet never, that themselves be deprived of their habitation there,
and therefore they desired that the Commissioners (they being their tributaries) to see they
have justice in the premises, the Commissioners
therefore, in regard the said Mr. Goodyeare is
not present, and that he is of New Haven jurisdiction, and at their Court, to hear to complaint
of the said Indians, and to satisfy the said
Indians if they can, if not to certify the Commissioners at the next meeting, the truth of

the premises; that some further order may be taken therein as shall be meet."

As the result of this emphatic protest by *Checkanoe*, and in evidence of its truth and fairness, we find that on the 27th of December following,[25] Captain Middleton and associates were obliged to satisfy the Indians, by purchasing Shelter Island, or as it was called by the Indians *Manhansick ahaquazuwamuck*,[26] from the Sachem *Yoco*, formerly called *Unkenchie*, and other of his chief men, among whom we find one called *Actoncocween*,[27] which I believe to be simply another descriptive term for our hero, for the word signifies "an interpreter," or "he who repeats," *i. e.*, "the repeat man."

This sale was certified to at Southold the

[25] East Hampton Records, vol. i. pp. 96–97.

[26] *Manhansick ahaquazuwamuck = Manhan-es-et-ahaquazuꝏamuck,* "at or about the island sheltered their fishing-place," or "their sheltered fishing-place at or about the island," see Brooklyn Eagle Almanac, 1895, p. 55, "Some Indian Fishing Stations upon Long Island."

[27] Compare Delaware (Zeisberger) *Anhuktonheen,* "interpreter, *Ekhikuweet,* "talker"; Lenâpé (Brinton)*Anhoktonhen,* "to interpret"; Otchipwe (Baraga) *Ânikanotagewin,* "interpreter," or "his work as an interpreter," *Anikanotage,* "I repeat what another says."

following spring,[28] but the deeds themselves
have long been lost, and the pages of the
volume on which they were entered despoiled
of their contents by some vandal years ago.
These items of record, however, point to one
conclusion, that if the owners of Shelter Island
were unable to produce Forrett's deed from the
Indians in 1652, which they seem to have been
unable to do, it is not at all likely that it will
ever be discovered.   It also indicates that
Forrett's title, as well as that of Mr. Goodyeare, rested on a frail foundation as far as
the whole island was concerned, and that the
Indians were right in their protest.

In this year according to tradition, or what is
more in accordance with facts, in the spring of
1653,[29] *Yoco Unkenchie* or *Poggatacut*, as he is

---

[28] Southold Records, vol. i. p. 158.

[29] The late David Gardiner in his Chronicles of East Hampton, p.
33, and other Long Island historians following him, place this event
in the year 1651 ; but as *Yoco*, as he is more often called, united with
the chief men of his tribe in the deed to Captain Middleton and associates on the 27th of December, 1652, a date which was, in accordance
with our present mode of computing time, January 6, 1653, would
indicate beyond question the error of our historians in assigning his death
previous.

variously named, passed away. The tribe, now without a head, and weak in tribal organization, migrated from Shelter Island. Some went to Montauk and to Shinnecock, while a few united with the Cutchogues. During the following three or four years much alarm was created from the rumor that the Dutch were endeavoring to incite the Indians against the English.[30] The conduct of the Montauks and Shinnecocks was such that they were particularly distrusted, and they were forbidden without special leave to come into the settlements.[31] It was forbidden to furnish them with powder, shot, or

---

[30] East Hampton Records, vol. i. p. 31 : "It is ordered noe Indian shall Come to the Towne unles it be upon special occasion and none to come armed because that the Dutch hath hired Indians agst the English and we not knowing Indians by face and because the Indians hath cast of their sachem, and if any of the Indians or other by night will come in to the towne in despit of eyther watch or ward upon the third stand to shoote him or if thay rune away to shoote him" (April 26, 1653).

[31] Southampton Records, vol. i. p. 90 (April 25, 1653) : "At a generall court Liberty is given to any Inhabitant to sell unto ye Sachem any manner of vituals for the supply of his family for a month's time from the date hereof, Mr. Odell haveing promised to use his best endeavors to see that the said Sachem buy not for other Indians but for his particular use as aforesaid." It is probable from the following note that this Sachem was Cockenoe.

rum ; nence we find but little recorded.   Again,
the war carried on between the Montauks and
Narragansetts began   in   this   year, and continued for some years with great loss on both
sides.   It is very doubtful if *Cockenoe* took any
active part in this war, or at least in its earliest
stages ;   for,   according   to   the   fragmentary
depositions by the Rev. Thomas James and
others,[32] in the celebrated *Occabog* meadows suit
of 1667,—a quarrel over a tract of salt meadow
located almost within sight of the village of
Riverhead, between the neighboring towns of
Southampton   and   Southold,—*Cockenoe* was
then residing at Shinnecock with his first wife,
the sister of the four Sachems of Eastern Long
Island, who united in the East Hampton con-

[32] East Hampton   Records, vol. i. p.   261 (Munsill's   History of Suf-
folk County, East Hampton Town, see Facsimile, p. 13), Extract : "and
the Shinokut Indians had the drowned Deere as theirs one this side the
sayd River and one Beare Some years since ; And the old squaw Said by
the token shee eat some of it Poynting to her teeth ; And that the skin
and flesh was brought to *Shinnocut* as acknowleding their right to it
to a saunk squaw then living there who was the old *Mantaukut* Sachems
sister ; And first wife to *Chekkanow.*"   In the trial November 1, 1667
(Colonial History of New York, vol. xiv. p. 601), an Indian testified :
" It was about fourteen yeares agoe since the beare was kill'd," which
indicates the year 1653 as the time the Saunk Squaw was living at
Shinnecock.

veyance. She was at this date, in consequence of the death of her brother *Nowedonah*, the *Sunck Squaw*, that is, the woman Sachem, of the Shinnecock tribe—a fact which proves that by marriage he came into the house of the Sachems, and was entitled to be designated as a Sagamore, as we find him sometimes called.

In the latter part of August, 1656,[33] *Wyan-*

[33] Hazard's State Papers, vol. ii. p. 359. As this record has never been quoted in full in our Long Island histories, and Hazard's work is quite rare, it would be well to print it at this time, viz.: "Upon a complaint made by *Ninnegrates* messenger to the Generall Court of the Massachusetts in May last against the *Montackett* Sachem for murthering Mr Drake and some other Englishmen upon ours near the Long Island shore and seiseing theire goods many years since and for Trecherously assaulting *Ninnegrett* upon block Island and killing many of his men after a peace concluded betwixt them certifyed to Newhaven by the Massachusetts Commissioners by a Complaints made by *Awsuntawney* the Indian Sagamore near Milford and two other western Indians against the said *Montackett* Sachem for hiering a witch to kill *Uncas* with the said Milford Sachem and his son giveing eight fathom of wampam in hand promising a hundred or a hundred and twenty more when the said murthers were committed; Notice whereof being given to the said *Montackett* Sachem and hee Required to attend the Commissioners att this meeting att Plymouth The said Sachem with five of his men came over from longe Island towards the latter part of August in Captaine Younges Barque whoe was to carry the Newhave Commissioners to Plymouth but the Wind being contrary they first putt in att Milford. The Sachem then desiring to Improve the season sent to speake with *Ausuntawey* or any of the western Indians to see whoe or what Could bee charged upon

danch, the Sachem of Montauk, with five of his men, on complaint entered against him by the Narragansett Sachem *Ninnegrate*, presented himself before the Commissioners, then in session at Plymouth, Mass. *Ninnegrate*, how-

him but none came but such as professed they had nothing against him; The Commissioners being mett att Plymouth; The said Sachem presented himselfe to answare but neither *Ninnegrett* nor *Uncas* nor the Milford Sachem appeared, only *Newcom* a cuning and bould Narragansett Indian sent by *Ninnegrett* as his Messinger or deputy charged the long Island Sachem first with the murther of Mr Drake and other Englishmen affeirming that one Wampeag had before severall Indians confessed that hee hiering under the *Montackett* Sachem did it being thereunto hiered by the said Sachem which said Sachem absolutly deneyinge and Capt Young professing that both English and Indians in those partes thought him Innocent : *Necom* was asked why himselfe from *Ninnegrett* haveing layed such charges upon the long Island Sachem before the Massachusetts Court hee had not brought his Proffe ; hee answared that Wampeage was absent but some other Indians were present whoe Could speak to the case ; wherupon an Indian afeirmed that hee had heard the said Wampeage confesse that being hiered as above hee had murthered the said Englishmen ; though after the said murther with himselfe that now spake the *Muntackett* Sachem and some other Indians being att Newhaven hee deneyed itt to Mr Goodyer and one hundred fathome of Wampam being tendered and delivered to Mr Eaton the matter ended : Mr Eaton professed as in the presence of God hee Remembered not that hee had seen Wampeage nor that hee had Received soe much as one fathom of wampam, Nor did hee believe that any at all was tendered him ; wherupon the Commissioners caled to the Indian for Proffe Mr Eaton being present and denying it the Indian answered there were two other Indians present that could speak to it ; they were called forth but both of them professed

ever, not appearing or submitting any proof of his allegations, *Wyandanch* was acquitted of the charges with much honor. At the same time he was relieved from the payment of the tribute, then four years in arrears, owing to his

that through themselves and from other Indians where then att New-haven yett the former afermined Indian was not there and that there was noe wawpam att all either Received or tendered soe that the long Island Sachem for what yett appeered stood free from this foule Charge ; 2 Cond, The said *Newcome* charged the *Montackett* Sachem with breach of Covenant in asaulting *Ninnegrett* and killing divers of his men att Block Island after a conclusion of peace, the Treaty whereof was begun by a Squaw sent by *Ninnigrett* to the said Sachem to tender him peace and the Prisoners which the said *Ninnigrett* had taken from the long Island sachem upon condition the said sachem did wholly submitt the said message, but afeirmed hee Refused to accept the Conditions which hee said hee could not without advising with the English whereupon the Squaw Returned and came backe from *Ninnigrett* with an offer of the prisoners for Ransom of wampam which hee saith hee sent and had his prisoners Relieved, *Newcome* affeirmed the agreement between the said Sachems was made att *Pesacus* his house by two long Island Indians deligates to the *Montackett* Sachem in presence of *Pesacus* and his brother and others, two Englishmen being present one whereof was Robert Westcott ; Pesacus his brother testifyed the agreement as afore-said. The *Muntackett* acknowlidged hee sent the said Delligatts but never heard of any such agreement and deneyed hee gave any such com-mission to his men, *Newcome* afeirming Robert Wescott would Testify the agreement aforsaid and desiring a writing from the commissioners to Lycence the said Wescott to come and give in his Testimony which was granted and *Newcome* departed pretending to fetch Wescott but Returned Not : The Commissioners finding much Difficulty to bring theire thoughts

distressed condition.   It is probable that *Cockenoe* was one of the five men accompanying him
on this occasion.

He again makes his appearance on record in
1657,[34] when he laid out and marked the bounds
of Hempstead in Queens County, by order of
Wyandanch, who had then acquired jurisdiction
as Sachem in chief over the Indians of Long
Island, as far west as Canarsie.[35] *" Chegonoe"*

to a certaine Determination on Satisfying grounds yett concidering how
Proudly *Ninnigrett* and how peaceably the *Montackett* Sachem hath
carryed it towards the English ordered that a message the contents
whereof heerafter followeth bee by Tho Stanton delivered to *Ninnigret[l]*
and that for the cecuritie of the English plantations on long Island and
for an Incurragement to the Montackett Sachem the two first particulars
of the order to hinder Ninnigretts attempts on long Island ; made last
year att New Haven bee continued ; Notwithstanding the said English
are Required to Improve those orders with all moderation and not by any
Rashness or unadvisednes to begin a broil unless they bee Nessesitated
thereunto ; The *Montackett* Sachem being questioned by the Commissioners concerning the Painment of his Tribute Professed that hee had
Pay[d] it att hartford for ten yeares but acknowlidged there was four
yeares behind which the Commissioners thought meet to respett in
respect of his present Troubles ; Plymouth Sept 17th 1656."

[34] Thompson's Long Island, vol. ii. p. 9.

[35] This protectorship was agreed upon and confirmed May 29, 1645, by
Rochkouw [*Yoco*] the greatest Sachem of *Cotsjewaminck* (= *Ahaquazu-
wamuck*).   See Colonial History of New York, vol. xiv. p. 60.   See also
Plymouth Colonial Records, vol. ix. p. 18.

witnesses the sign manual of his Sachem, who was present, on the confirmation deed of July 4, 1657.[36] This deed is dated 1647, as given in Thompson's History of Long Island.[37] The mistake is again repeated in Munsill's History of Queens County,[38] and has been often quoted by others quite recently ; but the date will be found correctly given in the Colonial History of New York.[39]

The records of Hempstead under date of March 28, 1658, read: "This day ordered Mr Gildersleeve, John Hick, John Seaman, Robert Jackson and William Foster, are to go with *Cheknow* sent and authorized by the *Montake* Sachem, to marck and lay out the generall bounds of ye lands, belonging to ye towne of Hempstead according to ye extent of ye limits and jurisdiction of ye s^d towne to be known by ye markt trees and other places of note to continue forever." These boundaries are named in the release of the following May, which " *Checknow* " witnesses. The appearance of his name

---

[36] Thompson's Long Island, vol. ii. p. 10.   [38] P. 145.
[37] *Ibid.*, p. 9.   [39] Pp. 416, 417.

on the records of Hempstead, and on these deeds, has led some writers to assume that he was a Sachem of the Rockaways,[40] an error which I find persistently quoted.

The year 1658 was a busy one for our Indian. The settlements are rapidly spreading and land is in demand by incoming colonists. On June 10 he laid out the beach to the westward of the Southampton settlement, giving Lion Gardiner the right to all whales cast up by the sea, and he witnesses the grant by his Sachem.[41]

On August 17[42] he marked out, by blazing trees, three necks of meadow for the inhabitants of Huntington, on the south side, in the western part of the present town of Babylon, which necks were afterward in controversy. The village of Amityville now occupies part of the upland bordered by the meadow. It states in the deed " that *Choconoe* for his wages, and going to marke out the Land shall have for

[40] Indian Tribes of Hudson's River, Ruttenber, p. 73 ; Munsill's History of Queens County, p. 19.

[41] East Hampton Records, vol. i. p. 48.

[42] Huntington Records, vol. i. pp. 16, 17.

himselfe, one coat, foure pounds of poudar six pounds of led, one dutch hatchet, as also seventeen shillings in wampum," which, together with pay for the land, "they must send by *Chockanoe.*" Our early settlers were always behindhand in their payments, and in this case, as evidenced by a receipt attached, pay was not received until May 23 of the next year, when Wyandance refers to "the meadow I sould last to them which my man *Chockenoe* marked out for them."

On April 19, 1659,[43] eleven years after the purchase, at an annual town meeting of the inhabitants of East Hampton, held probably in the first church that stood at the south end of the street,[44] *"It was agreed that Checanoe shall have 10ˢ for his assistance in the purchase of the plantacon."* Seemingly a dilatory and inadequate reward for such a service. Money, however, was very scarce and worth something in those days, and we cannot gauge it by the light of the present period. In comparison we can only

[43] East Hampton Records, vol I. p. 156.
[44] *Ibid.*, p. 66.

refer to the fact that Thomas Talmadge at the same period was only paid 20ˢ, or double the amount, for a year's salary as Town Clerk. The record, however, is a valuable one, and is one of the straws indicating the esteem and favor in which *Cockenoe* was regarded by the townspeople of East Hampton.

That *Cockenoe* took an active part in marking the bounds of the tract of land between Huntington and Setauket, now comprised in the town of Smithtown, presented to Lion Gardiner by *Wyandanch* on July 14, 1659,[45] as a token of love and esteem in ransoming his captive daughter and friends from the Narragansetts,

[45] Book of Deeds, vol. ii. pp. 118–19, Office of the Secretary of State, Albany.   The original is now in the possession of the Long Island Historical Society : "Bee it knowne unto all men, both English and Indians, especially the inhabitants of Long Island : that I *Wyandance* Sachame, of *Pamanack*, with my wife and son *Wiancombone*, my only sonn and heire, haveinge delyberately considered how this twenty-foure years wee have bene not only acquainted with Lion : Gardiner, but from time to time have reseived much kindness of him and from him, not onely by counsell and advise in our prosperitie, but in our great extremytie, when wee wee were almost swallowed upp of our enemies, then wee say he apeared to us not onely as a friend, but as a father, in giveinge us his monie and goods, wherby wee defended ourselves, and ransomd my daughter and friends, and wee say and know that by his meanes we had great comfort

is worthy of note, for it is evident that the Sachem had no one else so capable. In confirmation of this surmise and my belief that he had a prominent part in all the land transactions of Wyandanch, my friend William S. Pelletreau, who is preparing the early records of the town of Smithtown for publication, has lately found recorded, in a dispute over the lands of Smithtown, a deposition taken down by John Mulford of East Hampton, dated October 18, 1667, which reads: "*Pauquatoun*, formerly Chiefe Councellor to the Old Sachem *Wyandance* testifieth that the Old Sachem *Wyandance* appointed *Sakkatakka* and

and reliefe from the most honarable of the English nation heare about us ; soe that seinge wee yet live, and both of us beinge now ould, and not that wee at any time have given him any thinge to gratifie his fatherly love, care and charge, we haveinge nothing left that is worth his acceptance but a small tract of land which we desire him to Accept of for himselfe, his heires, executors and assignes forever ; now that it may bee knowne how and where that land lieth on Long Island, we say it lieth betwene Huntington and Seatacut, the westerne bounds being Cowharbor, easterly Arhata-a-munt, and southerly crosse the Island to the end of the great hollow or valley, or more, then half through the Island southerly, and that this gift is our free act and deede, doth appeare by our hand martcs under writ." Wayandance's mark represents an Indian and a white shaking hands.

Chekanno[46] to mark out the said *Rattaconeck* [*Cattaconeck*] lands, and after that ye s^d *Pauquatoun* saw the trees marked all along the bounds and the Sachem being with him, he heard him [the Sachem] say it was marked right. And there is a Fresh pond called *Ashamaumuk*[47] which is the parting of the bounds of the foregoing lands from where the trees were marked to ye pathway." This "Fresh pond" was at the northwest bounds of the town of Smithtown.

At the same time and year, probably, as it bears no date, he witnessed the sale of "Old Field" by *Wyandance* to the inhabitants of Setauket in the town of Brookhaven.[48] Also about the same time the sale of "Great Neck or *Cattaconocke*,"[49] bounding Smithtown on the east as referred to by *Pauquatoun*.

[46] These two chief men of the Montauk tribe were frequently sent together by *Wyandanch*, and were possibly the Delegates sent to *Pesacus* at Rhode Island as stated in Note 33. *Sakkataka* or *Sasachatoko* was at one time chief counselor of the Sachem of the tribe. He was still living in 1702–03, as the Montauk conveyance of that date bears witness.

[47] See Brooklyn Eagle Almanac, 1895, p. 55.

[48] Brookhaven Records, vol. i. p. 16.

[49] " The Name of the Neck aboves'd ; is *Cataconocke*, March 8 1666 "

On February 10, 1660,[50] he marked out, and also witnessed the confirmation of the sale of Lloyd's Neck, in the town of Huntington, by *Wyancombone*, the son and heir of the late Sachem *Wyandanch*, who had passed away, and whose son was then acknowledged by both the Indians and whites as the chief Sachem of Long Island. His name on this copy of a copy is misspelled as *Chacanico*.

In the confirmation deed for Smithtown, dated April 6, 1660,[51] by *Wyancombone*, the land is stated to have been laid out by some of the chief men of the tribe ; these men are named in *Pauquatoun's* testimony. In the copy recorded in the office of the Secretary of State at Albany, N. Y., *Cockenoe* is named as a witness in the corrupt form of *Achemano*. He united on August 16, 1660,[52] with the rest of his tribe

(Brookhaven Records, vol. i. p. 16). The Indian name, of which "great neck" is probably a popular translation, signifies "a great field," *Kehte-Konuk*.

[50] Huntington Records, vol. i. p. 20.

[51] Book of Deeds, vol. ii. p. 118, office of the Secretary of State, Albany, N. Y.; George R. Howell in Southside Signal, Babylon, June 30, 1883.

[52] East Hampton Records, vol. i. 172.

at Montauk, in the first Indian deed to the inhabitants of East Hampton for "all the afore[sd] Necke of land called *Meantaquit*,[53] with all and every parte thereof from sea to sea."

About this time the *Meantaquit* Indians petitioned the Commissioners of the United Colonies of New England for protection from the cruelty of the Narragansetts[54] with the result that the latter were ordered not to come within six miles of the English plantations, and the former not to begin any new quarrels, but to behave themselves quietly, without provocation. The fact that *Cockenoe* was then living at Montauk is proof that he must have been one of the petitioners.

Thomas Revell, a merchant of Barbadoes, and a resident of Oyster Bay, L. I., was engaged with Constant Sylvester, one of the owners of Shelter Island, together with James Mills of Virginia,[55] and John Budd of Southold, in the

---

[53] " The Signification of the name Montauk," Brooklyn Eagle Almanac, 1896, pp. 54, 55.

[54] East Hampton Records, vol. i. p. 175 ; Southold Records, vol. i. p. 363.

[55] Southampton Records, vol. ii. pp. 14, 20, 209.

West India trade. Through his partners, or otherwise, he became well acquainted with our friend *Cockenoe*, and employed him as an interpreter in buying some land from the Indians in Westchester County, N. Y. We find that Cockenoe was with him at Manussing Island, at the head of the Long Island sound, where he gave Revell a deed, witnessed by John Budd and others, dated October 27, 1661, which reads: "I *Cockoo Sagamore* by vertue of a full and absolute power and order unto him and intrusted by *Mahamequeet* Sagamore & *Meamekett* Sagamore & *Mamamettchoack* & Capt. *Wappequairan* all Ingines living up Hudson River on the Main land for me to bargaine & absolutely sell unto Thos Revell . . . And fardder more I doe promise and ingauge myself in behalf of the prenamed Ingaines & yᵉ rest of those Ingains which I now sell this land for and them to bring suddenly after yᵉ date hereof, for to give unto Thomas Revels or his order quiet and peacable possession," etc., etc. This tract of land thus conveyed was in the present township of

Mamaroneck, Westchester County, N. Y. The power of attorney given to *Cockenoe* by these Indians reads : " One of our Councill *Cockoo* by name an Ingaine the which we do approve of and do confirm whatsoever the said *Cockoo* shall doe in bargaining and selling unto Thos Revell of Barbadoes," etc. This power of attorney by some means was dated two weeks after the execution of the deed, and in the litigation which ensued over the purchase this fact ruined the case for Revell. This deed and the power of attorney were both recorded at Southampton, L. I.,[56] and are quoted in full, with particulars of the suit, in Sharf's History of Westchester County, N. Y.,[57] and are too lengthy to dwell upon at this time.

Cockoo, Cokoo, Cockoe, or *Cakoe,* as his name is variously given in the papers relating to this affair, is evidently an abbreviated form of *Cockenoe.*[58] All the facts recorded in connection with it point to him and to no one else. From

[56] Southampton Records, vol. ii. pp. 15, 16.
[57] See Mamaroneck, by Edward Floyd DeLancey, Esq.; chap. 23, pp. 850, 851.
[58] See Note 18.

the context of the papers, he was a strange Indian, not living up the Hudson river, where it is stated all the other Indians dwelt. That he was acting as an interpreter is evident—a fact which, as I have before observed, was a very rare qualification for an Indian of that period. Humphrey Hughes, whose name appears as one of the witnesses on Cockoo's power of attorney, was a seaman in the employ of Revell, and in his various capacities as a sailor, trader, fisherman, or an inhabitant, is frequently mentioned in the records of both South [59] and East Hampton towns; [60] hence *Cockenoe* was no stranger to him. Two years afterward Hughes witnessed the renewal of the Montauk Squaw Sachem's whaling grant to John Cooper ; therefore, taking all these items of fact into consideration, it is not at all strange that *Cockenoe* should have been employed by Thomas Revell in buying land from the Indians in Westchester County.

On February 21, 1662 [61] (February 11, 1661)

[59] Southampton Records, vol. ii. pp. 14, 15, *et seq.*

[60] East Hampton Records, vol. i. pp. 159, 160, *et seq.*

[61] From the original in possession of the owner of Montauk, Frank Sherman Benson, Esq.

Chekkonnow again united with his tribe in the
deed known as the " Hither Woods " purchase,
" for all the piece or neck of land belonging to
Muntauket land westward to a fresh pond in
a beach, on this side westward to the place
where the old Indian fort stood, on the other
side eastward to the new fort that is yet standing, the name of the pond (Fort Pond) is
Quaunontowounk on the north, and *Konkhonganik* on the south," [62] etc. At this date,
as is proven by the above wording of this deed,
the Montauks were encamped at the southern
part of East Hampton village [63] under the pro-

[61] *Quaunontowounk* = *Quaneuntⱷunk* (Eliot), " where the fence is,"
and refers to the "sufficient fence upon the north side of the pond."
Compare " the Indian fence at *Quahquetong*," Trumbull's Names
in Connecticut, p. 58 ; *Konkhonganik* " at the boundary place,"
Kuhkunhunkganash, " bounds" (Eliot), Acts xvii. 26. The agreement,
Book of Deeds, vol. ii. p. 123, office of Secretary of State, Albany,
N. Y., dated October 4, 1665, says : " That the bounds of East Hampton to the East shall be ffort Pond, the North ffence from the pond to
the sea shall be kept by the Towne. The South ffence to the sea by
the Indyans." *Askikotantup*, daughter of the Sachem Wyandanch, was
Sachem Squaw of Montauk at the date of this agreement.

[62] This passage reads : " The cruel opposition and violence of our
deadly enemy Ninecraft Sachem of Narragansett, whose cruelty hath
proceeded so far as to take away the lives of many of our dear friends
and relations, so that we were forced to flee from the said Montauk for

tection of the settlers, in order to escape the invasions of the Narragansetts, and Montauk was temporarily abandoned.

In the same year *Checkanow* was sent with *Tobis*, another Indian, by order of the *Sachem Squaw*, widow of *Wyandanch*, to mark out John Cooper's whaling limits on the beach to the westward of Southampton.[64]

Some of the boundaries of Huntington, laid out in 1658, being disputed by their neighbors of Oyster Bay, it became necessary to send for *Cockenoe* that he might identify his former marks. At a town meeting held at Huntington March 8, 1664[65] (26–12–1663). "It was voted that when *Chiskanoli* come that Mr Wood shall have power to agree with him, and the town to gratifie him to show the boundaries of the necks of meadow at the south bought by the town."

---

shelter to our beloved friends and neighbors of East Hampton, whom we found to be friendly in our distress, and whom we must ever own and acknowledge as instruments under God, for the preservation of our lives and the lives of our wives and children to this day."

[64] East Hampton Records, vol. i. p. 199.
[65] Huntington Records, vol. i. p. 58.

In the following spring[66] "Att a Generall
meeting of yᵉ Deputyes of Long Island held
before yᵉ Governer at Hempstedd, March 6ᵗʰ
1664 (March 16, 1665), It is this day ordered
yᵗ yᵉ Towne of Huntington shall possesse &
enjoye three necks of meadow land in Controversy between yᵐ and Oyster bay as of Right
belonging to them, they haveing yᵉ more anncient
Grant for them, but in as much as it is pre-
tented that *Chickano* marked out fouer Necks
for Huntington instedd of three, if upon a
joynt view of them it shall appeare to be soe,
then Huntington shall make over the outmost
neck to Oyster bay," etc.

In the affirmation by John Ketchum and
townsmen, who went with Cockenoe to these
meadows according to the foregoing order of
the assembly, we find the following interesting
record:[67] "When wee came to the south to
our meadows wee went ovar too neckes to our
naybours who had called *massapeege* Indians,
About the number of twentie, whoe opoased us
About the space of an ower and would not

[66] Huntington Records, vol. i. p. 58.   [67] *Ibid.*, p. 90.

suffer the Indian [*Cockenoe*] to goe and shew us the marked tree, then we show the Sachem [*Tackapousha*] the writing to which hee had set his hand which was our acquitance, and yet hee would not suffer the Indian to goe, when wee see nothing would prevaile, wee took our leave of them and said wee would carry backe this anser to them that sent us; but they not willing that wee should, tooke up the matter as wee did apprihend spake to the Indians whoe after gave leave to the Indian who was *Chickemo* to goe and shew us the tree, many off *massapauge* Indians went with us. Thomas Brush went before and not taking notise off the tree went past it then a *massapauge* Indian called him backe and shewed him the tree before *Chickenoe* came neare it, when *Chickenoe* came to the tree hee said that was the tree hee marked, as his master Commanded him. *Massapauge* Sachem said by his Interpriter that hee told *muntaulke* Sachem that hee was grived at his hart that hee had sould that necke upon which then wee was, but *muntalket* Sachem tould him that it was sould and it could not bee helped and therefore bid him goe and Receve his paye and so hee said hee did: and alsoe *massapauge* sachem owned his Land and that he had Receved the goods."

Thomas Topping of Southampton and William Wells of Southold, two of the Deputies, who were in Huntington at this time by order of the Assembly,[68] "touchinge three necks of meadowe, wh^ch Huntington had formerly purchased of *Muntaukatt* Sarchem, and he informs true properiet^y as also in responsion to Oyster Bay inhabitants, who lay a claime to part of the said three Necks, saying thare are fouer necks & one thereof belongs to them, the said *Chickinoe* now did playnly and cleerly demonstrate before them that the Tree he first marked by his Master *Muntakett* Sachems order, and hath a second tyme denied according to order, is noe other but that wh^ch ought justly to be owned by him and soe marked as aforesaid, and comprehends only Huntingtons just Purchase of three Necks of Medow and in truth is three necks of medowe & not four according

[68] Huntington Records, vol. i. pp. 91, 92.

to the present relation of *Chickinoe.*" The Huntington men, it seems, were rather greedy, and *Cockenoe*, true to their interest, and having been "gratified," was trying to give them all they claimed.

The *Massapeag* Sachem *Tackapousha*, who has put on record "that it grived his hart" to make this sale, was a thorn in the flesh of the settlers of these two towns as long as he lived. It was utterly impossible to satisfy his demands, The records show that both the English and Dutch were obliged to buy him off time and time again.[69]   He is one of the most selfish and turbulent characters we find in the whole aboriginal history of Long Island.   Had he and his tribe been more powerful than they were, they would have left a bloody page on the annals of Long Island ; as it was, it was his weakness alone that prevented it.

On November 3, 1669, at East Hampton, before the Rev. Thomas James and others,[70] "*Checkannoo*," with other chief men of the

---

[69] Colonial History of New York, vol. xiv. Index, under Tackapousha.
[70] *Ibid.*, p. 627.

Montauk tribe, made an acknowledgment in "utterly disclayming any such vassalage as *Ninecraft* did declare to the Governor at Rhoad Island & doe protest against it in our owne names & in the name of ye rest of ye Indians at Montaukett & doe further declare that he shall have no more wampom of us without approbation of ye Governour of this place & that we acknowledge ye Governour at New Yorke as our chiefest Sachem."

The same year, with his associates, *Cockenoe* [71] gave a certificate that many years before they heard the old Sachem Wyandanch declare, in a meeting of the Indians, that he gave to Lion Gardiner and Thomas James all the whales which should come ashore, at any time, on Montauk. [72]

On December 1, 1670, [73] together with *Poniuts*, alias *Mousup*, grandson of *Wyandanch*, and other chief men of the tribe, "*Chekonnow*"

[71] East Hampton Records, vol. ii. p. 33.

[72] The date of this gift to Gardiner and James was November 13, 1658. See East Hampton Records, vol. i. p. 150.

[73] From the original deed in possession of Frank Sherman Benson, Esq. There is an imperfect copy in Ranger's Deeds of Montauk, 1851.

joined in the Indian deed for the land between
the ponds, to John Mulford, Thomas James, and
Jeremiah Conkling. This conveyance took in
all the land to the southward of Fort Hill between the " Ditch plain " and the " Great plain,"
and is remarkable for its Indian names of boundary places.[74]

By an entry of July 4, 1675,[75] *Cockenoe* was
one of the crew engaged by James Schellinger
and James Loper of East Hampton, as the
record states, "uppon the Designe of whalleing
. . . During y[e] whole season next ensuing,"
then a growing industry on the south side. This
service included the carting and trying out of

[74] These boundaries are as follows : " bounded by us, the aforesaid
parties [*i. e.*, the Indians] *Wuchebehsuck*, a place by the Fort pond, being
a valley southward from the fort hills pond, *Shahchippitchuge* being on
the north side, the said land, midway between the great pond and fort, so
on a straight line to *Chabiakinnauhsuk* from thence to a swamp where
the haystacks stood called *Mahchongitchuge*, and so through the swampe
to the great pond, then straight from the haystacks to the great pond, so
along by the said pond to a place called *Manunkquiaug*, on furthest
side the woods, growing on the end of the great pond eastward, and so
along to the sea side southward, to a place called *Coppauhshapaugausuk*,
so straight from thence to the south sea," etc. See Indian Names in
the Town of East Hampton, Tooker, East Hampton Records, vol. iv.
p. i–x.

[75] East Hampton Records, vol. i. p. 379.

the oil at some convenient place, for which the crew were to receive, "one halfe of one share of all profit what shall bee by us gotten or obtained During ye said terme of time."

The Indians of Long Island were disarmed in this year on account of King Philip's war, and on October 5 [76] *Mosup* the Sachem, grandson of *Wyandanch*, with *Pekonnoo* [an error for *Chekonno*], Counselor, and others, made supplication by a letter written by Rev. Thomas James to Governor Andros at New York, "Alledging the fact that they had always been friends to the English and their forefathers before them, and this time of war fighting with the English Captains, desired that their guns might be returned, as it was the usual time of hunting." Owing to an indorsement on the back of this letter, written a week after by James, on mature consideration, the request in its entirety was not granted. [77]

[76] Colonial History of New York, vol. xiv. pp. 699, 700.

[77] James wrote: "The lines upon the other side I wrote upon the desire of the Sachem & his men, they were their owne words & the substance thereof they also had expressed before Mr Backer, but since my writeing of them wch was almost a week since, I perceive that

On June 23, 1677,[78] *Cockenoe* appeared before
Governor Andros and Council at New York, in
behalf of the inhabitants of Hampstead, who
were having trouble with the Indians in their
neighborhood, regarding land laid out by him
in 1657, twenty years before, to which I have
previously referred. At the same council he
interpreted the speech of *Weamsko*, the Sachem
of *Seacotauk* in Islip, who claimed the *Nesquak*
[*Nissequogue*] lands; also the speech of *Swa-
neme*, who pretended to own the land called
Unchemau [Fresh Pond] near Huntington. In
the copy from which this has been taken he is
called *Checkoamaug*, an evident error of some
transcriber.

We find him occasionally employed by the

delivering up the armes to the Indians doth not relish well with the
English, especially since of late we heard of the great slaughter, they
haue made upon the English in other parts of the country; I perceive att Southampton ye English are much troubled ye Indians haue
their armes & I thinke it doth much disturbe ye spirits of these haue
them not ; as for these Indians for my owne part I doe thinke they are
as Cordiale freinds to the English as any in ye Country & what is
written by ym is knowne to many to be ye truth, though God knows
their hearts," etc.

[78] Colonial History of New York, vol. xiv. p. 728.

proprietors of Montauk, especially in the year
1682, when he is "*paid* 9ˢ *for keeping the
Indian corne*,"[79] and as much "*for burneing
Meautauk*,"[80] which was done every spring to
free the land from underbrush and weeds.

The years are now rapidly fleeting, and
Cockenoe is advancing in years with the settlements.   The power of the Montauks is a thing
of the past ; they exercise no control over
the rest of the Long Island Indians, who con-
vey land without the assent of the Montauk
Sachem.   As most of the younger generation
of the natives can speak English, probably as
well as he, there is no necessity for him to interpret.   He is now about the last of his generation still exercising the right as a member of
the house of the Sachems, in the councils of the
clan ; and, on August 3, 1687,[81] he unites once
more with the members of his tribe in the Montauk conveyance to the inhabitants of East
Hampton : " For all our tract of land at Man-

[79] East Hampton Records, vol. ii. p. 109.
[80] *Ibid.*, p. 111.
[81] The originals of the Montauk Indian deeds are in the possession of
Frank Sherman Benson of Brooklyn.

tauket, bounded by part of the Fort Pond, and Fort Pond Bay west; the English land south by a line from the Fort Pond to the Great Pond . . . to the utmost extent of the Island from sea to sea," etc., and then he retires from our view forever on the records of the past.

At the time of making this deed, half a century had elapsed since the conflict on the hills of Mystic—fifty eventful years in the history of our Colonies. If he was twenty-five years of age when he parted from Eliot in 1646 or 1647, he had then reached threescore years and five; not by any means an aged man, but, for all we know, he may have lived for some years afterward.[82]

There may be other recorded facts relating to his life which I have overlooked, or they may lie buried in the time-stained archives of other Long Island and New England towns—

[82] As his name does not appear among the grantors on the confirmation deed for Montauk, dated March 3, 1702–03, we must accept it as sufficient evidence that he had passed away before that date; although his associate and companion *Sasachatoko* was still living, an aged man. Rev. Thomas James died June 16, 1696, after a ministry of about forty-five years.

inaccessible, undecipherable, and unpublished—
which some future historian may unfold and
bring to light.[83] The seeds of knowledge planted
by Eliot on the fertile field of this native's mind
bore good fruit, even if his preceptor did write
at an early day he knew not what use he then
made of it. For the part he took in the rise

[83] It is to be regretted that we have left us so little relating to the Rev.
Thomas James and his knowledge of the Indians of Montauk. The few
depositions and letters he left show that his knowledge of Indian tradi-
tions and customs must have been quite extensive. In September, 1660,
he informed the Commissioners of the United Colonies, then in session
at New Haven, that he was "willing to apply himself, to instruct the
Indians" of Long Island, "in the knowledge of the true God." An
allowance of £10 was therefore made for him "towards the hiering of an
Interpreter and other Charges." In 1662 he was paid £20 "for Instructing the Indians on Long Island," and the same allowance was continued
for the two following years. In a letter from Governor Lovelace to Mr.
James (Colonial History of New York, vol. xiv. pp. 610–11, we find :
" I very much approve of yor composure of a Catechisme. . . That wch
I shall desire from you at p'sent is the Catachisme with some few select
chapters & Lauditory Psalms fairly transcribed in the Indian Language
wch I will send over to England & have quantityes of them printed & if
you thinke it necessary I conceive a small book such as shal only seme to
the instructing ye Indians to read may likewise be compiled & sent with
them," etc. The Catechism referred to above was probably never
printed (Pilling's Algonquian Bibliography, p. 569). It cannot be possible that James neglected to avail himself of *Cockenoe's* knowledge.
The facts presented in this paper would indicate, from James' reference
to him, that he found him a valuable assistant for many years.

and development of our settlements—a life work, unparalleled by that of any other Long Island or New England Indian—he deserves to be enrolled upon the page of honor. And now, amid the rolling hills of Montauk, which he loved so well, and within sound of the everlasting murmur of the mighty ocean, which he so often heard, in a grave unmarked and unknown,[84] he sleeps to await the resurrec-

[84] The numerous valleys and hilly slopes of the " North Neck," to the northeast of Fort Pond, are dotted in many places by Indian graves. The pedestrian will meet with them in the most isolated spots ; but generally near swamps and ponds in proximity to wigwam or cabin sites. The two principal are located at " Burial Place Point," on the eastern shore of Great Pond, and on the top of Fort Hill. The outlines of the Fort still visible (which was yet standing in 1662) now inclose forty graves, each marked by cobblestones laid thickly along the tops. The tramping of cattle has obliterated all traces of mounds, and the stones are generally on a level with the surface. On the outside, in close proximity to the others, are ten more, while on the slope of the hill to the northwest—the hill not being so abrupt in its descent at this point—are eighty-six more graves ; making a total of one hundred and thirty-six buried on this hill. All are marked in the same manner, the last being covered by a thick growth of blackberry vines and bayberry bushes, and would not be noticed by the careless observer. One of the graves, inside the outlines of the Fort, has an irregular fragment of granite for a headstone ; on it is carved very rudely $\frac{1817}{B\,R}$. This is evidence that the graves on this hill were all subsequent to the erection of the Fort, and

tion morn. A scarred and battered fragment from nature's world—a glacial bowlder, typical of the past—should be his monument[85]—on one side a sculptured entablature, inscribed :

" *To the Memory of a Captive in the Pequot War, the first Indian Teacher of John Eliot; A firm friend of the English Colonists; Cockenoe-de-Long Island.*"

are not very ancient. Those at "Burial Place Point" look much older, and some of the graves there are simply depressions not marked by any stones. In the "Indian Field," to the northwest of Great Pond, are many more.

[85] I would suggest placing this at the top of Fort Hill, and thus preserving the hill and graves forever as a memorial.

THE END.

www.ingramcontent.com/pod-product-compliance
Lightning Source LLC
Chambersburg PA
CBHW021528090426
42739CB00007B/837